THREAD

D1445754

ALSO BY MICHAEL PALMER

BOOKS AND CHAPBOOKS

Company of Moths
Codes Appearing
The Promises of Glass
The Danish Notebook
The Lion Bridge: Selected Poems 1972–1995
At Passages
An Alphabet Underground
For a Reading
Sun
Songs for Sarah
First Figure
Notes for Echo Lake
Alogon
Transparency of the Mirror
Without Music
The Circular Gates
C's Songs
Blake's Newton
Plan of the City of O

SELECTED TRANSLATIONS

Voyelles by Arthur Rimbaud
Jonah Who Will Be 25 in the Year 2000 (film by Alain Tanner)
The Surrealists Look at Art (with Norma Cole)
Blue Vitriol by Alexei Parshchikov (with John High and Michael Molnar)
Theory of Tables by Emmanuel Hocquard
Three Moral Tales by Emmanuel Hocquard
in *The Selected Poetry of Vicente Huidobro*
in *The Random House Book of Twentieth Century French Poetry*
in *Nothing the Sun Could Not Explain: 20 Contemporary Brazilian Poets*
in *Twenty-two New French Writers*

OTHER

Code of Signals: Recent Writings in Poetics, ed. Michael Palmer

MICHAEL PALMER

THREAD

A NEW DIRECTIONS BOOK

ACKNOWLEDGMENTS: Many of these poems first appeared in the following publications: *Alaska Quarterly Review, American Poet, Big Weather, Poems of Wellington, Boston Review, Columbia: A Journal of Literature and Art, Court Green, Crowd, Cue, Dragonfire, Eleven Eleven, Festschrift for Clayton Eshleman, Fulcrum, Lana Turner, Maggie, Miracle of Measure Ascendant: Festschrift for Gustaf Sobin, The Nation, NO: A Journal of the Arts, Paul Revere's Horse, Poem in Your Pocket, Public Space,* and *World Literature Today.*

"The Classical Study" first appeared, with a pastel by Irving Petlin, from The University Libraries at the State University of New York, Buffalo, and in *Company of Moths.*

"Aygi Cycle" was first published as a limited, fine press edition, with Dutch translations by Tom Van de Voorde (Druksel, 2009).

A selection of poems from *Thread* has been published in a single copy *livre d'artiste*, designed, hand-lettered and illustrated by Wesley Tanner, entitled *What I Did Not Say* (Passim Press, 2011).

Manufactured in the United States of America
New Directions Books are printed on acid-free paper
First published as New Directions Paperbook 1200 in 2011
Published simultaneously in Canada by Penguin Books Canada Limited

Library of Congress Cataloging in Publication Data

Palmer, Michael, 1943–
  Thread / Michael Palmer.
    p. cm.
  Poems.
  ISBN 978-0-8112-1921-1 (pbk. : alk. paper)
  I. Title.
  PS3566.A54T57 2011
  811'.54—dc22

                    2011000211

10 9 8 7 6 5 4 3 2 1

New Directions Books are published for James Laughlin
by New Directions Publishing Corporation
80 Eighth Avenue, New York 10011

Contents

THREAD

THREAD

WHAT I DID NOT SAY

The Classical Study

I asked the Master of Shadows
wherefore and wherefrom

but he said that art was short
and life was long.

Said: let us praise
those flames that consume the day

stone by stone
and the lilac by the barn

and the hours when you were young
and the mother- and the father-tongue.

Curled by fire the leaves of grass,
buckled, the roof beam,

shattered, the wagon's haft,
ash-flecks in the wind's swell.

Have you forgotten the whistling of the stones,
the heave and shift of the windrows?

So I asked the Master of Shadows
about the above and the below,

the this and the that,
the first and the last,

but he said,
I am no master

only a shadow,
and he laughed.

The Classical Study (2)

"Blessed the bell"
Baudelaire

I asked the Master of Shadows
wherefore and wherefrom

and he replied, I sell
insurance in a tiny town

and know-not-up
from know-not-down.

My head is a cracked and pitted bell
or only the crack within the bell

and I've lost my reflection
down the town well.

Will you lend me a bucket
to get it back,

then lend me a hat for that second head
and a ship to sail to the Quadrant of Dreams

and a dream to savor in the mean?
For I am the Virgin of Invisible Ink,

famed Laureate of Lyric Deceit,
shadowless snowman in the tropical heat,

a game that can't be won.
My theory is that time is done.

The Classical Study (3)

The Master has forgotten his hat.
Without his hat he cannot fly.
Without his hat his dreams escape
up.

Without his hat he cannot tip
his hat to that woman passing by
whom he remembers
from somewhere, as in a dream,

a room in a dream or maybe a beach,
a beach by the sea,
blindingly white,
hatless, he and she.

The Classical Study (4)

I asked the Master in Rochester
how far the music would carry us.

Past the eglantine, the briars and the bloodgrass?
Past the power station in flames, Martyrs' Square,

and Suleiman's Gate? Past the desert snows
and the Arctic sands? Past the missing pages

piled up in dark basements? The mummified hawks?
I asked in the language of sparrows, of

weasels and owls and gem-studded pharaohs
whose gaze is level and calm.

I asked the Master in Rochester
how far the body would carry us.

Past the donut shop and the Lubyanka and beyond?
I asked as we ordered coffee for the journey ahead.

But first a round of billiards,
the Master said, to settle the nerves,

a game where silence matters
above all, or do I mean sound?

The Classical Study (5)

I found the Master on Shijo-dori
at a steamy pachinko parlor.

He wore an abstracted look,
the eyes half glazed, jaw slack.

Pulling a squeezebox from his ever-
present sack, and pointing back,

he said, These dudes are masters
of the game, the bells and the bling,

the ching-a-ling-ling,
you must commit your verses to the flames.

Then he began to play, stray bits
of the old songs, from another day,

Blue Moon, The Blue Room, Blue Rain,
Blue Skies, Blues in the Night,

others I couldn't name.
An accordion, he said,

what moans and sighs it emits,
song and counter-song

at war in the violent air.
And finally with his twisted smile:

Tin Pan Alley, man,
stop me if you can.

The Classical Study (6)

I asked the Master among
the buildings of Bricktown
where my future lay.

Eyes rolling up, he replied,
Your fate is the same
as the buildings of Bricktown,

the children, the streets,
the stray dogs of Bricktown,
the spike-heeled whores

and slim hustlers of Bricktown.
Your words are the same
as those spoken and sung

by the citizens of Bricktown.
The sundry sights you see
you see through the windows

and doorways of Bricktown,
among the alleys of Bricktown,
by the river's ruined shore

wending through Bricktown.
Don't search for your face in that tide
or for a skiff to ferry you out to sea.

Memorize its streets
and study its walls.
One severed song fits all.

The Classical Study (7)

Dixit Magister:

I am Orphée today
Orpheus né Morpheus
far above and well below

the lid of sleep, lip
of earth, curl and
jerk of severed limbs

adrift among the
bent-backed reeds
headless, sleepless Orphée today

silent Orfeo who sings
to feral dogs and winds of change
to sleet and mud and empty space

The Republic of Dreams

She lay so still that
as she spoke

a spider spun a seamless web
upon her body

as we spoke
and then her limbs came loose

one by one
and so my own

The Late Discretion of J. V. Foix

That poem I dreamed last night
No need to write it down

A Mistake

I mistakenly killed a man some years ago. I do not mean that I killed him by mistake, since I killed him intentionally. I mean that it was a mistake to kill him. I slit his throat with a serrated hunting knife I then always carried. It was in front of a Chinese laundry on Manhattan's Lower East Side. I thought he had called me "little dago boy," though in fact, as others later attested, he had called out, "Hey, little day-glo boy," in playful reference to the bright color of my shirt.

Difference

You answered the phone and said
I am not at home.

No, you answered the phone
and said

João Cabral is not at home.
A difference.

Difference (2)

Answering the phone
Cabral would say

João Cabral
is not at home.

I don't know—
he's gone

perhaps never
to return.

Difference (3)

There is no more
a João Cabral

that one who wrote
of lucid spindles,

fragile threads,
that one who wrote

of stone, in stone
So he intoned

Difference (4)

You should
know

that I
wrote

my final
poem

some time
ago

a perverse
piece

of antiverse

The Cord

To whistle or whisper
To breathe along the bone

To twist the torso so
(That we drink the grey water)

To loose the limbs
(That we bathe in their dust)

To laugh, just as monsters must—
mouths open, tongues taut

To itch and to scratch
just as monsters must

To trace the sleeve of praise
against the liquid dark

To elevate our offerings
of burnt flesh and mint

(Line the windcaves
with panther skins)

To see voices yes
under light's duress

To conduct the streaming pit
(That we live in it yes?)

for C.E. at 70

L'Azur

I returned a book to John Ashbery last week. It was 1" × 1" × 1", a perfect cube. "Gee, Michael, you've had that book for twelve years. What took you so long?" "It was surprisingly dense," I answered, "almost as if nine-tenths of the universe's dark matter were packed inside. Also, that azure cover put me off for a good while. I thought it might be a Symbolist work, something about swans and ice, and you know how I've detested swans ever since that incident ..." "Did she ever recover?" asked John. "Out-wardly she's fine, but, really, she's never been the same." "Well, I'm not entirely myself today either," said John, "but I'm happy to have that book back. I've always liked that strange title. What do you think it means?"

What I Did Not Say

What I did not say was that within this tiny book, this 1″ × 1″ × 1″ cube, there was but one word. It was not even an unusual word, rather one people once used all the time as a call or a greeting, mornings or evenings, or else to express a certain delight, for example in the color of a lover's eyes or the grace of his or her form. A word, then, with no specific referent or single meaning, one often simply meant to intimate concord or mutual understanding, agreement or solidarity. This word had been banned from public utterance for many years, but it had subsequently, as often happens, worked its way back into common parlance until the point where the ban itself became a subject of ridicule, and those who had imposed the ban were reviled, where formerly they had been cheered and celebrated. Is it possible to conceive that this almost invisible book, with that one word in it, may have been responsible for this turn of affairs?

When the dancer

When the dancer split in half, we envied her that. When the halves be-
gan to dance, we applauded that. When the dancer pierced the wall, we
marveled and clapped. When the dancer danced down through the floor,
we were astounded by that. When she terminated time, we rose as one.
When she dove through glass, we tipped our collective hat. The shards
on the floor gleamed with an unnatural light. She bowed and she smiled,
then exited in a flash, stage left and stage right.

for E.S.

The Counter-Sky

A young woman of the book
directed my gaze toward the counter-sky

Behind her there were books piled up
miles and miles of books piled high

and below the scholars bent to their tasks
reading by the light of green-tinted lamps

I stared at the coffee in my cup
the coffee in my empty cup

and asked, "Would you like
a sip of coffee from this cup?"

And she said yes, and drink she did
from my cup's perfect emptiness.

I Fell Asleep

I fell asleep while reading, but the story continued. I ironed a shirt in my room, a thousand shirts in my room, then put one on, sky blue. I descended to the hotel veranda, took the slender hand of the widow Christa Train, and onto the frozen bay we danced. We danced out to the ship caught in the ice, hull stove by the ice, deck tilted to the west, mainmast snapped, name in gold lettering, The Young Republic, still visible on the uplifted stern. Perfect silence enveloped the ship.

When the ice had first closed in and taken its grip, he remembers, the ship had emitted heaving groans and sharp cracking sounds. Eventually these diminished in intensity, then subsided entirely. What had at first been a source of great curiosity for the shore dwellers quickly became a matter of indifference, a thing scarcely noticed. After stripping the ship of its goods and witnessing its slow demise, people had grown almost apathetic toward the looming remains, however impressive the shadows they cast upon the ice in the changing winter light.

We danced round that ship, we two, danced and danced back toward the shore, the veranda, the hotel, the lamps, though by then we were out of step.

for Howard Norman

It Is True

It's true that we'd met
and in meeting we'd laid the bet,

the bet had been placed on the table
We said what we did not mean

to say,
that test we designed,

the cleaving of signs
amidst the litter of crusts,

of petals and pots and cups,
their cracks and chips

silent witness, sufficient testament
to what

Say

Say she is the Queen of Bollywood, of special seeming
and tell us too that Mr. Speakes is silent
and how the tattoo master, Tuttle,
is Caravaggio for our time.

Say that the music we heard
was a real thing
formed of ebony and earth
and unrehearsed

and that it caused the drama on the screen
to swell
making the unreal come to be
in ways we could only envy.

Tell us what we most and least
wanted to know
of who and what we are
beneath, right now.

for Gustaf Sobin

Say (2)

Say that an old man in his garden
considers the mysteries of clover and vetch

while a helicopter passes overhead
scything the afternoon air.

Say that he has known these things before:
clover and vetch, helicopter and the ditch

again and again into which people fall.
His memory is perfectly clear

and serves no good, no purpose
at all. He has seen things before

(the fly in the bottle,
the indeterminate will).

Santa Muerte, Saint Death,
we pray to you to swallow our breath.

Say (3)

Say that a poem—this one—
has disappeared

and a figure of wilder grace
wide of eye, long

of limb and hair
has taken its place

Say that her body sways
to a different, wordless

music, and that her thoughts
cannot be fathomed

or perhaps she has no interest—
puts no trust—

in thought at all
Let there be that music then

retuning the evening air
till she too disappears

Say (4)

Say that Ariadne spins the Nine Songs,
spins and sings them, the first
for the body, the second for the prey,
the rest for the seconds, the minutes,
the hours of the day, the month's weeks,
the years' flight, the thread of lives,
the call along the pitch-dark corridors.

Say it is the body in time she spins,
the body on a singing bridge
and it is the dark she spins,
the lovers in the dark
enlaced by time and confused by the dark
and the secret at its heart.
And if it rains here in Knossos

as in other places and times,
and if the comet's tail,
on clear nights, hangs
above the water in the eastern sky,
and if indeed the lovers say nothing
as they speak and as she spins,
say nothing twice and twice again

one moment to the next, one note
in Knossos as evening comes,
as hesitant night descends
with no meaning and no art to it,
then perhaps the one song
will suddenly make some sense
and if not we can pretend.

Say (5)

Say that a spider with a death's-head
crawls into your bed
and offers to make love.

How explain
that you are done with love?
And what of death?

Poem, don't be so strange.

Say (6)

Say
that whatever comes
goes.

The Shadow knows
nothing,
such

his calling.
Round his
listing

house
the bindweed
grows.

We await

We await the *angelos*, the messenger. Is it the blind woman robed in ochre silks, gold hoops piercing her ears, her jet-black guide dog beside her? The young Latina with the deep-eyed child on her lap? The hip-hop master? The blond girl with braces and backpack and violin case? The withered, white-haired man, his face covered in fresh bruises? The driver of the tram? The slender nurse in white shoes and cap? I ask my companion Bei Dao, seated beside me, who it might be, but he gives no answer. You may wonder about the name of this city we are weaving through by tram, whatever city it is we are in.

Red C

I asked the Master of Silence
why he rode horseback with the Cossacks

and he said, to peer
into the Eye of Heaven,

perhaps through the eyes of death.
I asked the Master of Silence,

a Jew, what he saw as he rode
and he spoke

of streetlamps and taverns and indolence,
watermills and ceaseless rains,

bright cherries in heaps, churches in flames,
slaughtered oxen and racing clouds,

bent women gathered by a well.
So daybreak and nightfall

and my silence.
No heaven awaits.

Move

Move that barn a little to the left
if you would

and that memory of a barn
a little to the right

until they coincide.
That's good.

That

That the sorrel's now full in its bed,
the lavender, thyme, the forget-

me-nots, all of a blueness
and greyness, the sage,

heartsease, artemisia. That the spider,
bright white, its dew-flecked

Assassin's Gate, stretches stalk to stalk.
This she tells me and more—

that wild parrots have nested
in the palm, mice in the ivy,

and at each cardinal point
a kind of murderous calm.

Fragment After Dante

And I saw myself in the afterlife of rivers and fields
among the wandering souls and light-flecked paths.

There I was amazed to find
the damned and the innocent

commingled so, torturers and victims,
masters, sycophants and slaves

idling arm in arm, chatting
about nothing, about the fullness and ripeness

of nothing, the pleasures of the day
and of the hearth fires to follow

in the evening calm.
And they turned to me as one

and I heard their words, their
calls, each syllable, each phrase

but could not make them out.
And I saw myself struggling to wake,

howling and foaming like a dog,
biting at empty air.

Second Fragment

And she clasped my arm and said,
You, my son, who have lingered

too long among the dead, go
and return to the lighted shore

for those brief moments you have left
there among the hypocrites,

the torturers and deceivers
who've locked our republic in their thrall

as I'm told, for that far
I cannot see from this clouded place.

Then before my eyes her face
transformed from old to young,

that one I'd known in earliest youth,
and disappeared from view.

Thought (Third Fragment)

It is no light or simple thing
as Dante reminds us

in Canto 32
to render the absolute

bottom of the universe
amidst the piercing wails

of those self-devouring shades
locked in a lake of ice

their twisted, puss-
filled mouths

spewing endless shattered words
up towards this shattered earth

Nam

My job in Nam was to kill snakes. I was a member of what was unofficially called Viper Unit. Our orders were to keep the base free of serpents, poisonous land crabs, anything of the sort that might present a threat. How I was chosen for this assignment was never clear to me. One day an officer approached as I was cleaning my M14 and informed me of my new duties. Instructions followed from a grunt whose tour was almost up. Special equipment was issued, including an anti-venom kit, though it was emphasized that there would be little danger as long as I adhered to the protocols.

We gave our prey various names: The Night Sky, The Singer, The Poet, Waltz Time. The Night Sky, after its markings, which reminded us of constellations. The Singer, with its bands of yellow, coral and black, named for the distinctive "singing" tone it emitted as it rippled by. The Poet, an iridescent, emerald creature with indigo accents—I can't remember how it got its name. And Waltz Time, since it was rumored that after three steps you would expire from its bite. All four were said by the locals to be edible.

My day done, I would often join a friend who worked in the truck pool. We would lay out under the tarp of one of the half-tracks and smoke opium together—his supply was seemingly limitless and always quite pure. As the ring of opium flared then dwindled around the pipe's bowl, I would doze off and dream not of home, but of snakes, brilliant-hued, graceful, fleet and elusive.

Gu Cheng

Nobody wishes for the name
of the nameless flower.

Nobody wants to hear
the untellable tale.

No one wants you to return
as the skeleton of a nameless bird

bright plumage shed
on its flight toward death.

Who cares to drink
from the overturned pail of hours

spreading its red stain
across the millet fields?

Who would turn the pages
of the one book, the unreadable book,

as curtains tremble in the early
breeze? Earth bearing us in circles,

bearing the hovels and palaces,
night herons and night jasmine,

the wave-skimmers, the dancers,
the lovers intertwined, the

tiny blossoms and toxic piles,
clocktowers and sentinel fires,

whirled round and round,
the caws and cries.

Bees (6/12/06)

What the poem knows
I know not

What the pen writes
I do not

What the page says
I cannot hear

in this din, this din,
this summoning, spiral

din, without, with-
in, this call, this hum

of bees among
the hawthorn's bright

mays today this
noise this day

of silent suicides
in ink-dark light

far off, far away
Add one to one

to conjure none
Add us to them,

impossible sum
of wind and sand,

chance and plan,
this din, this hum

of day turned night
and green undone

After Hölderlin

Straws of the world we are,
wind-tossed, ignited, lost

sojourners, stranded mariners, babblers
among the bright towers

here where the City
of Industry sleeps

and flares, seabirds
circling in attendance,

night herons, shearwaters, petrels
beyond the hawsers and the harbor lights,

the wave-crests, carrion and rust.
One must wait.

One must wait
to draw a night song from these names,

the then and the now, the dark and light
as they alternate, just out of reach.

Untitled (Oct 06)

An unremarkable house like Spinoza's
seems perfect in form,
its steeply pitched roof,
four chimneys, shutters open,
bare winter elms, worn
slender path before the door.
True that he and his lathe
did not stay long
in this house near Leiden.
True as well that it
tells us nothing, being
of brick and perfectly silent,
perfectly finite and fixed.
He lived there for a while
and moved on.

Plato's Dirty Poem

Plato's dirty poem
certainly should have been banned,
cast into Hades' flames
following Plato's plan

To Say the Least

It is curious, to say the least. I have been to countless poetry readings over the years, some I'm certain very good, many of course not. Yet I have no memory of any of them. The ones I do remember with absolute clarity are those that for a particular reason or other I failed to attend. Illness, inclement weather, my car malfunctioning (a broken clutch cable once), paralyzing depression, reluctance to engage with a crowd (even a small crowd), simple forgetfulness, disillusionment with the art, a minor social obligation, what have you. I remember each of these events and my absence from them in the finest detail. One stands out above the rest, a posthumous reading given in San Francisco by Ezra Pound, his first appearance in that city. Many hundreds of course were present; it had been a source of fevered speculation for weeks in the community and even in the popular press. But I did not attend. I stayed home and drank a little red wine with a light supper while reading Nerval. Then I went to bed early and dreamt, I recall, of a sundered and silent paradise.

Violet If You Will

"I like a guy who can quote Hegel over breakfast," said my Aunt Violetta, Violet if you will, elegant, long of limb, still youthful. "You know, 'Minerva's owl spreads its wings with the falling of dusk,' thereby transforming morning into twilight, and the two fried eggs on your plate into an owl's yellow eyes." "As for Hegel," she continued, "as I need hardly add, it is not his monstrous dialectic that attracts, that metaphysical abomination, but his fugitive metaphors, signifiers of an intense and immediate desire, desire at breakfast and at nightfall. These render him readable, and this is what your mother, dry as toast, never came to understand, and it is the principal reason I refused to attend her during her final, hallucinating hours."

Violet Continued

Violet continued, "I meant simply that the only meaningful history is played out in the violet hours, those unmeasured and unmarked hours just outside of time, the story—the history—that occurs outside of history, history as desire, Hegel's other side."

Broad Waking

Slant from the poem's mouth
Atlantis arrives, the cries
of children arise, the dance
begins, perfect circle of the
squared poem, its cardinal
points, stillness and motion
and the singing against time,
the dancing in time,
the ringing in our ears,
the silence as the waters rise

Madman with Broom

The realist crows return
at earliest morning.
And the madman with broom,

madman in his nightshirt
with a broom, he too returns.
He thinks to roust the crows

from the mulberry boughs
by jabbing and swirling his broom,
by crazily twirling his broom

in the wet summer air
and hurling curses skyward
beyond the boughs and the crows

towards the fading gods among the fading stars.
But the realist crows know
it is only a man

in a nightshirt after dawn,
that the broom is a broom
and that his cries are nothing more

than words and half-words
the heavy air will swallow.
They rise anyway from the tree

as best to quiet him
and let morning be morning.
Soon enough they'll return again

by twos and threes, settling among
the spreading limbs, their laughter the same
before and after.

Hiddenness

(Kansai plains)

To enter the temple we had to pick the locks,
put off our shoes, sing to sleep the clocks
watching us.

Peel your skin back
from the top
and pass through the chamber of clouds,

of peonies, elms and pale herons,
of emperors long dead
therein assembled,

the silent, the wild-eyed,
the meek and the violent,
the awkward and the graceful dead

therein assembled.
Entering the temple the rain will follow
and come to rest

there, above your head.
It will lave memory,
it is said,

then ask its one question.
About the hours,
their parts?

A space of time, might we say,
that a glimpse
will not contain?

Count the silent stones
if you can
and the ringing drops.

Bridge of Bones

A child is running across a bridge of bones.
A woman calls to him, but he doesn't listen,

a tall woman with flowing hair.
He is chasing an unknown creature,

dark and small. The water is rising,
skimming the bridge's underside.

She keeps calling to him,
calling him by a private name

as he crosses the bridge in the waning light.
The bridge's bones are oblong, hollow, bleached white,

and lie side by side lengthwise,
a flute of sorts, in the wind

where the beast, the child and her cries
disappear, there among the cypresses,

the cedars and ferns
at bridge's end. In another life

she is the lover of the child.
She lets her dress fall from her shoulders,

calls him by a private name,
feels the singing bones beneath her feet.

Poem Against War

She raises both arms
to free the clasps binding her hair

View

Little
left of

us here
on this

mountain
of gold

Coloring Song

I'd like
a life

of cobalt
blue, very

dark, very
deep blue.

What does
this mean,

what does
it mean?

Nothing at
all, nothing

at all.
And you?

Aygi Cycle

And here the rains
think little of us

their music is such
and the wind is such

and "the time of ravines"
the tiny wild orchids

in the damp fields
Night again

and the life-book
writing itself

Aygi Cycle (2)

Our walk then by sea's edge,
land's westernmost edge,
and the waves' violent crests
that day, when my despair noticed
the shifting, the silent migration
of the dunes, and you
the low alyssum flowering white,
artemisia, hence Artemis, her
rites, speaking as we walked
of things other than we thought

Aygi Cycle (3)

So the bright
cadmium fields
of wild mustard

and the dark crows'
eternal arguments
and we wonder

if the poem
if the poem will unfold
toward them

and the coiled voices
their summonings below

Aygi Cycle (4)

Coarse hawthorn
beloved uncle's
memory entwined

among its
gnarled and
armored limbs

copy of
Lolita by
his deathbed

Aygi Cycle (5)

Within the small poem time
and tales of the preening gods
among the sliding stars

and love's silent
mirror held up
to the crimes of war

within the small poem

Aygi Cycle (6)

Invisible
between tree and field
that nothing

zero *zephirum* that wind
whirling leaf
wind

between tree and field
wind—wind of paradise?—
that zero nothing zephirum

Aygi Cycle (7)

The late ice
begins to sing
in the winter
of Aleksander Blok's

great poem *Twelve*
and now here
outside the poem
beneath the eaves

Aygi Cycle (8)

This house
so known

and not
the late

wind plays it
at times

tunes it
at times

to what
slant pitch

recalls its
voices lost

their tones
sudden laughter

brittle rage
as though

on a
burning stage

Aygi Cycle (9)

There at horizon's lip
hurtling clouds

of deepest red
over tiny, listing ship

and I a passenger
by a different name

Aygi Cycle (10)

Spare light
of this world—
not entirely
of this world
not entire

Cooper's Hawk
dining on a sparrow
in the pepper tree's
thick, aged limbs,
feathers floating so

slowly down
to the moist
earth below—
O book
of bleeding branches

Japan: Inland Sea

That poem
left out in the mist
now illegible

Transit

(after Wellington)

God's eye
in a paua shell
plucked weeks back
from the violent tides

of Breaker Bay,
resting now be-
tween Ha Jin's
War Trash

and Creeley's *On
Earth*, his last,
on a simple shelf.
We've come

to the old
echoes again,
swallowed songs,
tongues of cloud and wind.

I know the word appears

I know the word appears
nowhere in your lexicons,
cannot be found
arrayed among the others
within the alphabet's
immutable order. Yet the poem
has called for this word,
insists upon its presence
as it told me
in a high-pitched, silent
voice very late last
night. For what other word
could possibly mean
"the lover's touch" and "the
widow's song" all at once,
"the stranger's glance" and
"the bullet's path" all at once?
"The illumined night," "the dark
of this waning day"?
And even as we speak,
this word, not-a-word,
seems to want to mean
still another thing.

Traumgedicht

At the Café Revolver they were playing Mahler.
No one was listening other than Mahler

himself, to my left. It is deeper than Strauss,
wouldn't you agree, he remarked

to no one in particular. He owns
the present but the future is mine. Outside

trams rolled among the bright shops
with their gilded facades

as the sudden drumming
of a hailstorm began.

Listen to that, Der Mahler said,
is not the unexpected always best?

Shall we throw dice
to see who survives?

Last Request

Bury me in a cocoa pod, it's time.
Bury me in a Mercedes Benz, a
silver one, I've met my end.
Bury me in a lobster shell, a

carapace of red, now I'm dead.
Bury me in a jet marked KLM,
a typewriter labeled Remington,
a stove-in boat, symbol of my clan.

Bury me in a pot of India ink,
only place that I can think.
Bury me in a skull in Voronezh
that dreams of dragonflies

and the spider's web, heaped
hills of human heads, since I'm dead.
Bury me in a can of flammable film
with Keaton (Buster) and Beckett (Sam).

Bury me in Little Boy and in Fat Man,
plunging toward the edge of time.
A cuckoo clock, a block
of bluest ice. Quincunx, Devil's Trill,

or 22 June, Town Hall, '45.
Lay me beside her in the Song of Songs,
our limbs forever intertwined,
now that I'm not alive.

Or plant me with the poets in an opium pipe,
its glowing ring of light.

Stick me in the ground
without a thought without a sound.

Passejo

Señor Muerte and I
go out ghostwalking together

How have we not met before
asks the one of the other

When Sancho

When Sancho wrote the *Quixote*
were agent oranges raining from the trees
of Sevilla, windmills dicing limbs
into edible bits?

Were there then such ovens as we've seen
for baking human bread?
Today, the gentle sun of early spring
on moist earth, purple hyacinths,

sudden sparks in the young girls' eyes,
plum in full blossom, and the
swallows again, the carrion crows
as ever. So soon it comes around,

Sancho, so tell me if you can,
who scratched the poem
along the charred walls
of the ancient corridors?

National City

I thought I would live in National City
forever, grow a beard, grow old,
hold close the dark secrets of the State,
the secrets of syntax, secrets of the dancer's
lithe memory of the body
in a space undisclosed, chamber
where light imitates time,
crossing as it does the bright tiles
to surprise us with an ending,
a muscular thought. Thought
that we might in the dark
fashion the lament of the speakers,
lament of the sleepers,
the sanctified cartoon.

THREAD

(Stanzas in Counterlight)

"Du labyrinthe aux deux entrées
jaillissent deux mains pleines d'ardeur."
René Char

Nighthawk and sun-bird
beauty of the world   beauty of the world

How can one write   *beauty of the world?*

Fumbled for each other in the dark
familiar, unfamiliar, the touch

of watery air
walls, weight   of watery air

cards scattered across a table,
game of chance they had played

So, Alyosha, maybe it is true
that we live in *perhaps*.
Perhaps the earth ... perhaps the sky ...
chemical winds, auroras, tides,
chalk hills and blistered pines
and the microtonal bells.

And those who swallow ink
(the ringers of bells),
perhaps they will inherit
the bogs and salt marshes,
the swamp grass and samphire,
jacket with torn pockets, shredded cuffs.

Will inherit the sea-foam, the dust,
the ferrous mud
that reabsorbs us.

From the Mercury Fountain, Mahmoud,
spills a stream
echo of things
sun to stone speaking
cicada to poppy
not milk of paradise
no river of stars in the dark
just the bent wheel of days
meaningless ripples in the heat

From the eyeless mountains, Raúl,
fall
voices beneath voices

We hear the hawthorn, the penstemon,
the goldenrod   even here

hawthorn and goldenrod
shadows of wheeling terns

mountains then sea
sea swallowing mountains

We hear. And we hear

the tongues of days, names
melting into sea

wavemouths, indifferent air

even here   lodestar
lexicon   *labyrinthos*

Along the corridors
of the invisible world, Raúl,

gardeners raise such flowers
as need no light

such flowers
watered by voices

as need no eyes
to be seen

It is the role of the lovers to set fire to the book.

In the palm garden at night they set fire to the book

and read by the light of the book.

Syllables, particles of glass, they pass back and forth in the dark.

The two, invisible—transparent—in the book,

their voices muffled by the book.

It is the role of the lovers to be figures of the book, the

illegible book,

changing as the pages turn,

now joined, now clawing the fruit from each other's limbs,

now interlaced, now tearing at throat and vein,

then splayfoot, then winged, then ember,

as the music of the book,

rustling through the palms,

instructs.

The moth, Robin,
we've both learned
at different times
from its motion, a
quantum of nothing
could we say,
dusk to dark morning
before full day,
a battering of wings,
night notes sounding
beyond our extinction

Circling lost
through the narrow streets
of the Old City
among the shuttered shops
they hear nothing
but the howling of dogs drifting down
from the hills above
from the dark
of the parched hills
threnos—thread—lament
barely vibrating web
of sleep's winding streets

(even
in
dreams,
Roberto,
the
police)

We must count in Babylon.
Surely in Babylon we must count,

count the days and the dead,
the chambers of the palace,

its stones, its steps, its
flaring lamps, must count

the clouds, the petals of the flowers,
the hours, we must count the hours

as they pass
so slowly for the young,

so swiftly for the withered
masters of this place,

ardent assassins of speech
hidden away. Surely

in Babylon we must count
the gardens tended, the towers raised

by slaves in this city
soon to be dust, count

the days and the dead.
Must we count the dust?

(after A.T., in the dark)

There must suddenly have come a
time come a moment late in life

when he desperately needed to write

books as a way
to survive in this life

books then more books
and so he wrote

of assassins and the night breeze
the ice-dancer and the sky-writer
the hang-glider who fell

so slowly before our eyes
(we averted our eyes

went on about our business
as the waves folded over him
mangy dogs patrolling the shore)

Wrote of himself and his double
playing cards at a table
covered in green baize

himself and his lover
violently interlaced

Wrote of torturers lighter than air
offering a tender caress

insects buzzing philosophy
(o Pascal o Marquis de Sade)

statues bleeding
from eyes

and mouths
of stone

infinite blacktop stretching out

infinite shredded ribbons of cloud

Wrote even while dying
of time erasing time

Nighthawk and sun-bird
Who will tell of it

Shore's eyelid, earth's rim
light from extinguished stars

bathing us
in time's wake

time's long
stream of slaughter

and song
Some love

the one more
some the other

Ave manes   a specter
appeared in my dream

a shade with vulture-bone flute
calling to his dead

his unwept unremembered
dead among the terraced

hills and stubblefields
his needlessly dead

in the rusting sands
his comically dead

with lolling tongues
(Lorca's fluted bones

threaded among the nameless)
the recent and the distant

wind and water tossed
dead stars beneath stones

in nomine patri
and of the son

and of the piping the signifying ghost
ghost of pentacles ghost of music halls

spider-legged spider-white ghost
his ancient broken unplayable flute

Under the sign of the alphabet
the rain fell up the
bodies in the quarry spoke
of the Lord's great hunger
and the Lord's blackened tongue

and they chanted the secret
names of the Lord
one by one

And the rain fell up the
bodies in the quarry danced
and the sky filled with sand
the color of rust

The blind boys sang
and the dead men danced
and the deaf men heard their chants

Under the sign of the appetites
a rustle of silk
the barest sound droplet of
ink off the blood moon's
faint glow
then ripple then stream
then river of ink
darkest ink invisible ink
flooding the clouds below
liquid hours below
liquid eyes dark as ink
and I dreamed we were still alive
dreamed we were not yet born
dreamed we were yet to be

From the Mercury Fountain, Mahmoud,
flow the tenses: past, present, future;
future-past, first and last, daily acts;
desires; angels of slaughter and syntax;
the zero and the zero plus one; deep eyes,
slender wrists; coffee and speech; sleeplessness
and its dreams; the meadow orchid
low within the grass; evening primrose;
cadence on the felt of the dice
so casually thrown; the tumbled stones,
the field of tolling flowers.

Tenses of the present, Mahmoud, the (im)possible
present, infinite presents threading
now forward, now back. Amidst the
shattered symmetries and scattered fictions,
between actual river and imagined shore,
actual breath of wind through the frayed,

half-open curtain
passing so
suddenly over them
those years ago,
brief flare of the lamp,
shadows that danced
upon a wall.

Gustaf, under earth
by the tiny grave-pits
Merovingian words we
speak by the plague wall
by the house of the suicide
by the Mount of Winds
sits the low house of stone
lies the silkmaker's house
thread spun and gone.
Words are the distant home.

Chimera, sightless stars have colonized the meadow

Chimera, helicopters are birthing their young into the waves

Language of the waves, Chimera, language
   of the owl,
      silent petrels by the salt shore,
      the plover repeating its note

Saw the singer in flames by the shore

Watched her swallow her song

Nowness in Neverland she sang

Watched the palace disappear beneath the sea

while a later world sailed overhead

Endless amusements of the cruise ship
with no origin or port of call

Saw the singer in that ink-dark dream

Neverness and nowness she sang

beauty of the world   broken world

she sang, Chimera,

such words the fire offered her